# A MESSAGE FROM MY FATHER

*James C. Clay Jr.*

PublishAmerica
Baltimore

© 2012 by James C. Clay Jr..
All rights reserved. No part of this book may be reproduced, stored in a retrieval system or transmitted in any form or by any means without the prior written permission of the publishers, except by a reviewer who may quote brief passages in a review to be printed in a newspaper, magazine or journal.

First printing

PublishAmerica has allowed this work to remain exactly as the author intended, verbatim, without editorial input.

Hardcover 9781462660902
PUBLISHED BY PUBLISHAMERICA, LLLP
www.publishamerica.com
Baltimore

Printed in the United States of America

# INTRODUCTION

I have chosen to write this book on behalf of the late James C. Clay Sr. He was a man that suffered much during the course of his life like so many before and after him. Even though his hardships and heartache were many he showed great character and resiliency gravitating toward good instead of the bad. Most people today choose to follow others down paths that are not suited for them but because people tend to gravitate towards the world they lose sight of what's really important in life.

My Father was a simple man. He wasn't someone that followed the norm or trend just to be on the side of everyone else. No, he was just the opposite. He was a man of courage and of wisdom. He sets a great example for those who lack self-control and find themselves under pressure to please people or things that are not important in God's plan. Pops didn't have a college degree or a six or seven figure bank account. He was not privileged at all. But what he had was integrity and honor. Because of these characteristics, "God, My Lord and personal savior chose him to be one to witness what everyone else wonders about, is there life after death." Now, beyond a shadow of a doubt I can truly say, "yes" there is definitely life after death. You will be surprised of who is there and who is not. The reason why is because of the integrity of the man that said it, "My Father". Dad experienced a brief moment in the tribulation period. He witnessed to souls that were waiting for judgment, souls he knew and recognized. I do believe more now than ever, "that Our Lord God is not a respecter of persons".

Matthew 7:13-14 [13] "Enter by the narrow gate; for wide is the gate and broad is the way that leads to destruction, and there are many who go in by it. [14] Because[a] narrow is the gate and difficult is the way which leads to life, and there are few who find it.

Many people try to hide what's in their hearts from God. "You can't. "You", will be responsible for all your actions whether you believe it or not. Many folk spend a life time chasing after things that will make them happy, only to wake up one day feeling an emptiness that can't fill with nothing other than Jesus Christ, "some realize it and some never do".

My Dad was really special. His legacy will live through me and others he has touch during his lifetime. He has shown me the true meaning of honor, character and integrity. The book describes where he came from and how he got to where he ended up. During his early years, I don't envy him at all. The racism that seemed to permeate the south during his era was extreme. Being black and poor was a double curse in the south.

My Mom was the pillar of strength for my Dad and family. "She wasn't always there the way I believe he wanted her to be there, but when it counted, she stood up for him like no other". To me she represents someone who benefited by being close to someone who was wise and driven to persevere no matter what challenges were in front of them. It's reflected by who she is today. I often tell Mom today she acts just like her husband. They exemplified the meaning courage and that "can do attitude". In the succeeding chapters ahead you will witness the courage of both my parents and get a glimpse of what we have to endure sometimes when you are born without a silver spoon in your mouth.

It's the choices we make that count when we are faced with adversity and trials that truly determine who we really are in life and where we will go.

# HUMBLE BEGINNING'S

My Great Grandfather was one of thirteen children. He was born as Thomas Henry Clay, a freed slave. His wife Sarah Milton was a white woman who came from a prominent family. Thomas and Sarah were married in October of 1893. Thomas was a business man and was well respected in the bayou country. He was born a slave to my great- great grandmother Ulalie. Ulalie was a concubine for a slave owner by the name of Alexandre Verdun. Ulalie gave birth to seven children for Alexandre in Jefferson Parish New Orleans. When Alexandre's wife realized he wasn't going to stop his relationship with Ulalie, she couldn't deal with the embarrassment any longer and left with her two children and was never heard from again. Upon Alexandre's death he left all his land and possessions to Ulalie and his seven illegitimate children. His land and livestock was split seven ways in which all received an equal share. Thomas learned a great deal about business from his father and grew his livestock. He began to barter his livestock for land. Within ten years he quadrupled his land holdings and livestock.

He moved to Terrebonne parish, southwest of New Orleans in 1890. His livestock was needed in the community and because his father was well-known through-out Louisiana, he was allowed to continue to grow in this way as long as he kept his place in the south (of black origin). He was well respected in the Terrebonne Parish area and because of his success I believe he thought he had overcome racial barriers because he traded with the whites and Indians in the area; not too many blacks were allowed to trade or do business with whites in those days. He truly was an exception.

He met Sarah one day while doing business in Houma during the spring of 1893. They started secretly meeting each other and she became pregnant. When she could no longer hide it knowing her family would never approve of her relationship and especially being pregnant by a black man, she had to make a decision. My great-grandfather knew at that moment if the whites found out he had fathered a child by a white women he would be sought after and killed. He also loved this woman tremendously and was willing to put his life on the line for her. They decided to wed. After the marriage they went deep into the bayou leaving everything they owned. For fifteen years they lived in the swamps of Raceland, Grand Calliou and Dulac Louisiana. They raised ten children. After the years of exile my great-grandfather decided to come out of hiding believing times had changed to reclaim his land and livestock. He discovered his holdings had been taken by whites and when he tried to legally get it back he was caught and hung by the neck in Thibodaux, Louisana. My great grandmother reached out to her family and she was disinherited by her family and never allowed to be a part of the family again. Sara took her children back to Dulac where she raised them and died in the early 1920's.

Back in the late 1930's on a small farm in Houma, Louisiana my Father was born. He was the second oldest and the first male child. Back in those days in rural areas where farming was prevalent children often started working at 2 to 3 years of age. He worked on the farm until he was able to go to school at age five. By his second year of school he had to stop his education to go work in the sugar cane fields in Terrebonne Parish to help sustain his family. He was seven years of age at the time he left school and never returned, even though it was promised to him that he would return one day by his father. Pops was a hard worker and never complained about anything. He had a strong love for his Mother and siblings. He became a bread winner for the family and his brothers and sisters always came to him for things they needed just like children come to their fathers. They grew up on the homestead east of Houma in a small town called Mechanicville. Mechanicville was a small town where poor blacks moved to acquire land that the government allocated as homestead property. Many of these families were born into debt, debt that was left by their parents. So a homestead would allow them to live on an artificial estate of land, created to protect the possession and enjoyment of the owner against claims of creditors by preventing the sale of the property for payment of the owner's debt's as long as the land was occupied as a home. Homesteading was a great asset for families back then who lacked basic reading & writing skills. Often they would enter into contracts and would have no way of verifying what was stipulated in the contract they entered into leaving them vulnerable to carpetbaggers and con artist.

My Dad's father was educated by the church. The church back in the 1920's was the only source of education for poor blacks and Indian children. In Louisiana Catholicism was the dominant religion during that time and would often provide religious classes for the children in the area. They were taught very basic reading and writing skills while learning about God and Jesus Christ. My Grand Father was a man who had the gift of open visions.

*Acts 2:17 And it shall come to past in the last days, says God, That I will poor out of My Spirit on all flesh; Your sons and your daughters shall prophesy, Your young men shall see visions, Your old men shall dream dreams. NKJV*

When my Grandfather passed away in 1990, I had no idea he had this gift and he was very popular amongst the religious factions in the area. Grandfather was often sought after to interpret bible scriptures and dreams. Many religious preachers and teachers would come by on Sunday nights to hear his interpretation of scriptures and his analysis of a dream.

My Father worked various jobs until his early teen years, taking his earnings home every week and giving it to his mother who would take care of the house hold. He was conditioned to take whatever was left after household expenses were paid, if there was anything left. He met my Mom in the mid 1950's, at the time he was seventeen and my mom was fifteen. They dated for a couple of years and he was nuts about his future wife. He struggled with the responsibility he had at home being a provider for his family at this time. His loyalty was split between my Mom and his family.

*His Mom (my grandma) would tell me stories about him when I was a young lad indicating how proud she was of him. She told me he was a very loyal person and how he would always seem to do the right thing even if it hurt or meant that he would go without. He was selfish when it came down to family. As a young man I didn't realize the impact those conversations would have on me in my later years.*

Dad & Mom planned to get married to and have children but just the opposite happened. I was conceived before they could get married and this disjointed all their plans. When my Dad found out Mom was pregnant he told grandma and asked her not to tell his father. He knew his father would have a fit of rage. One day dad came home from work as usual and he entered the side door of the house, my grandfather was sitting waiting on him with a shotgun pointed at him. He cursed at my father and told him you are going to go and tell the parents of that girl you got pregnant and that you are going to get married next week no if's, ands, or buts. He immediately went to my Mom's parents and told them. Since they had no money saved up and neither wanted to stay in the same house as their parents they found a little sharecroppers cabin. The cabin was very small, dingy, poorly ventilated and right across the street from my dad's parent's home (If you know my mom you know that just wasn't going to last for long). Needless to say they were struggling and my dad was now trying to take care of two households which meant he would have to find a job that paid more money or find another job and work two.

# DREAMING OF A BETTER LIFE

Reverend Charles Inwood wrote that "When God is going to do something wonderful, he begins with a difficulty."... When he is going to do something miraculous, "He begins with an impossibility." God loves to defy odds, accomplish the impossible, operate in the supernatural, and amaze us with His creativity and power. We serve a big God—not one that is confined and limited to our understanding and our ability to figure out His ways

On March 15, 1958 my parents were married. The two families came together for the celebration and it was a bittersweet moment in our family history. Mom's family suffered a great loss because she kept her siblings in line while her mother and father were out working. She was the oldest female of ten children in the household and the responsibility of caring for her siblings was instrumental in maintaining order in the household. Her loss meant her Mom (my grandma) would have to cut her hours as a maid to care for her children. That was a big pill to swallow because they were struggling to make ends meet financially.

Genesis 2:24 Therefore a man shall leave his father and mother and be joined to his wife, and they shall become one flesh. NKJV

Even though grandma couldn't stand her job, she needed the job to put food on the table and hopefully get a few hand me down clothing from her employer for her children. Food and clothing were very hard to acquire when you made maybe a dollar a day and you had to feed and clothe ten children. My father came from a similar situation.

One day my father came home from work in June of 1958 expecting to see his wife and how much more she had swollen with a growing baby inside of her. He entered the front and only door and found his wife gone. He went across the street to see if she had gone to his parent's house maybe to sit and talk to his brothers or sisters. His family told him they hadn't seen her all day. He wasn't worried because he thought maybe she went across the bayou to visit her family. At about 9:00 pm he thought to himself maybe I better go and pick her up. He got out of bed and got dressed and went over to his in-laws to pick Mom up. He pulled up at about 9:20 and knocked on the door and my auntie Judy came and let him in. He asked where is Barbara (my Mom)? Judy replied and said I haven't seen her all day. She went to ask grandma and she answered I haven't seen her. He immediately left the house telling everyone he was going to the hospital thinking maybe something happened with the baby. Seven minutes later he was at Terrebonne General Hospital's emergency room inquiring about his wife. The intake person checked the hospital records and told him there wasn't anybody there by the name of Barbara Clay. He then went back to his parent's house and sat talking to his Mom until 1:00 am and then he went back home. The next day he went to work and at lunch time he went over to his in-laws again to find out if his wife showed up and the answer was no. Now everyone was worried. Grandma knew something fishy was going on so she called all her children one by one into the living room and drilled them with a series of questions. She knew one of them knew something about their sister's whereabouts because they were all very close. When that didn't work she drew her favorite licking stick which seemed like a half of a tree when I was a young lad. She starting whipping them one by one and finally Norma-Jean, "Mom's" middle sister said she got five dollars not to tell anyone she had gone to Detroit, Michigan. "Wow!" Grandma said "She went where?" Now my dad felt abandoned and really didn't know which way to turn. He left the house crying and confused not knowing what to do or how to even contact her.

It's early June in 1958, a young lady pregnant with me steps off the train and takes a huge sigh of relief. She was in awe as she looked around at the huge buildings that surrounded her in downtown Detroit, Michigan. The cars, buses, and people and all other movements put her in a state of happiness. She was excited about the opportunity to change her life forever and was looking forward to the challenges ahead of her. "Many people never understood how strong willed she was and often wondered why she always defied the status quo. The lord had a plan for her life and she knew it. Stepping out on faith many considered it to be foolish but she was always a woman of faith and bold as a lioness".

*Isaiah 43: 1-2 But now, thus says the LORD, who created you, O Jacob, And He who formed, O Israel: 'Fear not, for I have redeemed you; I have called you by your name; You are mine. When you pass through the waters, I will be with you; And through the rivers, they shall not overflow you. When you walk through the fire, you shall not be burned; Nor shall the flame scorch you*

Mom had contacted her mother's sister Ruby Mae, before she left Houma to insure a place to stay in Detroit until she could get on her feet. On her way to her new home from the train station she was hoping my dad would follow. She was really missing her husband more than ever, she wanted him to see the sights in Detroit and all the big city had to offer. Not knowing, how she was going to break the news to him really weighed on her but she knew if she hadn't made the move to leave she would have been stuck in Houma and that was not the kind of life or future she saw for herself or her children. When she arrived at Ruby-Mae's house late that evening there was a message for her to call her Mom. Knowing she wasn't going to take a step backward by going back to Houma, La., she was ready to battle with her Mom. After a short conversation, Grandma told her she was going to get my father so that they could all talk and try to resolve the situation. Grandma knew she couldn't change her daughters mind and she was hoping her new son-in-law could. An hour later they all were on the phone. Dad asked why did you leave and not tell me where you were going? Mom's response was I told you I didn't want our child to grow up in a place where black folk had to hold their heads down when a white person was walking by or where we couldn't sit on the bottom floor level of a movie theatre because of our skin color. Before he said another word she hung up the phone. When he heard the click he burst out in tears and he really didn't know what to do. His mother in-law said don't worry son, she was always strong willed and believe me when I tell you, you two will be ok, so go home and rest and we will talk tomorrow.

# REUNITING THE NEW FAMILY

The next morning dad awoke to the birds chirping away and the sun beaming through the window. He decided not to go to work that morning and decided to go across the street to visit his mother. When he entered into the kitchen where she seemed to be the better part of the day she look at him and saw the hurt and anguish on his face and said, "Son what's wrong and why aren't you at work?"

"He looked at her with tears in his eyes and said, Mom my wife left on a train yesterday and went to Detroit." I don't know what to do. "Grandma looked at him and said son let her go." You have responsibility's here. She will come back, who is going to want her with a child on the way. Anyway she was never right for you in the first place. I don't know what you saw in her from day one. For the first time he realized his wife was right. My mom told him many times that she felt very uncomfortable around his family and that she knew his family would do anything to keep them from moving away and starting their own life. She never told him of the snide remarks that were always being slung at her when he wasn't around because she knew they would deny it first of all, and that he wouldn't listen and would shut down instead. He never sided with her and always defended his family and their actions even if he knew they were wrong. He felt foolish and empty and he realized that he betrayed the trust of the one that really mattered.

He looked at his mother and said, "I am going to her. I can't let her be out there alone and unprotected." His mom interjected and said, "I think you are making a big mistake if you go to her" he responded "I don't care what you think because I have to do the right thing by her and my child." He leaned towards his mom to kiss her and she pulled away in disbelief with a look of shock on her face. She said, "You are going to leave your brothers and sisters and everything you know for her!" He responded and said, "Yes because I know that's what God would want me to do as a man." He quickly exited the house and went back to his house across the street.

He entered into his closet where he kept his money. He hid his money behind a broken piece of crown molding, not even my mom knew about it. Every week when he was paid from his job he would take five dollars and put it in his hiding spot and would give the rest to mom to take care of the household. He always saved for a rainy day. He pulled the money out and counted one hundred and fifty dollars. He knew that wouldn't be enough and decided to sell his car. It was a 1952 Buick Rivera. He owned it for two years and it was his prize possession. He kept it clean and it was the talk of the neighborhood. He went to the gas station where he worked and told his boss (Mr. Dupree) he's not coming back and that he was moving up north to Detroit and hoping to land a job in a car factory. Mr. Dupree hated to see him go and said, "you are the best employee I ever had and I hate to see you go." Mr. Dupree led him into the office and gave him thirty dollars his wage for the week and then said, "here is a little bonus" and handed him another thirty dollars and said, "good luck." My dad turned to him and said, "do you know of anyone that might want to buy a car?" His boss said how much you want for it? He shrugged his shoulders and replied "I don't know. I paid $500.00 two years ago but I put a lot of work into it." Mr. Dupree turned to him and said, "I might know an old man down the bayou in Pointe-aux-Chenes who might be interested. I will let you know tomorrow, you stop by ok," "yes Sir," he replied. He got in his car and drove across the bayou to Houma where his in-laws resided to speak with his mother in-law. When they saw him pull up they ran out to greet him. My mom's brothers and sisters were very fond of my dad and they all felt his emptiness. He told them of his plan to leave as soon as he sold his car to gather a few more dollars for the trip. My mom's brothers and sisters emptied their pockets and came up with ten dollars. They offered it to him but he declined and said, "I will be alright and thank you for the offer." They all went inside the house and they told him how proud they were of him making the decision to leave and wished they could go with him. My uncles and aunts all expressed their distain of the southern way of life and all said they know it must be more to life and how they were all tired of being treated like second class citizens. He sat and talked about the journey he was about to embark on and how he had hoped that God would be with him and would guide him. After a few hours of talking and eating he went back across the bayou to his family's home. School was letting out for the day and he wanted to tell his younger brothers and sisters he was going to be leaving soon. He knew they would take it hard because in many regards he was like a father to them. When he arrived he called all his brothers and sisters outside. When they came out, his youngest brother said," we heard you were leaving," and he "replied yes I am." Another brother said, "you know when the old man (Grandpa) gets home he is going to be pissed," and my father replied and said, "I have to do what I feel I am led to do, it's just the right thing to do. I just wanted to let all of you know that I love you and I am going to miss you." They all stood around him and tears started flowing from each one of their eyes, saying please don't go but he stood firm and said "I have to." It was truly one his darkest days. Everything he had every known he was walking away from because it was the right thing to do.

The next morning he climbed out of bed and started packing. His brother Melvin came over to help him pack. Melvin told him how angry granddad was and how badly he spoke of my father. After they got all packed up dad went back to the gas station to see Mr. Dupree. When he pulled up to the gas station Mr. Dupree came out to greet him, "son have you changed your mind about leaving?" Dad looked at him and said, "No." Dad asked, "Did you find a buyer?" Mr. Dupree said, "Yes." He went on to tell him he couldn't get three hundred. Dad asked, "Well how much?" Mr. Dupree said, "The man only has two-hundred fifty dollars and asked, would you be willing to take that." Dad stood and thought about it for a minute and then replied, "Yeah I'll take it." They went inside and completed the business transaction. Dad knew he just got ripped off, but he actually felt a since of freedom and was looking forward to being re-united with his wife. Mr. Dupree gave him a ride back to his house after they conducted business and said, farewell to my dad and wished him the best and said, "if you decide to come back and you need a job come and see me." Pop's looked at him and said, "I won't be back but thank you." They shook hands and parted. He went inside his house and looked around and made sure he packed everything he thought he needed. Once he checked and double checked, it was about 2 o'clock in the afternoon. He went next door to his neighbor, Cornell's house and asked if he could get a ride to the greyhound station first thing the next morning and his neighbor replied, "Yes I can take you at about five o'clock a.m. on my way to work." They shook on it and dad thanked him and left to go across the street to his mom's house to spend his last evening with her before departing the state the next day.

The next morning, Cornell knocked on the door at four forty-five a.m. He picked up a couple of bags and took them to the car. Dad told his mom the night before he was going to leave his keys in the mailbox and asked if she would give them back to the owner of the property, she agreed to do so. He grabbed the last bag, his keys, and walked across the street to mailbox placing the keys inside and proceeded to the car. They arrive at the bus station at five o'clock that morning. He had to wait until six o'clock for the bus station to open. When it opened he purchased a ticket to New Orleans train station.

When he arrived in New Orleans he called his mother-in-law to get the phone number to her sister's house in Detroit where my mom was temporarily residing. Once he got the phone number he went and purchased a one-way ticket to Detroit. The next train wasn't leaving for another two hours. He decided to sit and pray asking God to protect him and to be with him on this journey.

*Joshua 1:9 Have I not commanded you? Be strong and of good courage; do not be afraid, nor be dismayed, for the Lord your God is with you wherever you go.*

A big smile erupted over his face and a sense of peace surrounded him and he was looking forward to once again embracing his wife determined to make a better life. As he boarded the train a short time later he turned back to take one last glimpse of New Orleans, he smiled and a feeling of courage and accomplishment overwhelmed him.

# A NEW BEGINNING

When mom arrived in Detroit she really had no idea of what to expect. All she knew is that her aunt wanted to help her in starting a new life. When she arrived at aunt Ruby-Mae's home she was given a small room on the second floor of the house. It was a big house. She had never seen a house with so many rooms and was in awe of what appeared to be what she had envisioned for her family. A little while later, while unpacking her clothes, she heard her aunt cussing up a storm in the basement. She went to see what was going on and discovered there were people on cots everywhere in the basement. Her Aunt was talking to one of the men as if he was someone who wasn't worthy of respect she thought to herself who have I moved in with. At that moment she realized that she and Ruby-Mae were going to butt heads. Mom was strong willed and so was Ruby-Mae who was used to getting her way and never hearing the word no. After listening to the verbal bashing for a few minutes she returned to her room and finished unpacking her clothes. After about an hour or so there was a knock at the door and it was Ruby-Mae husband. She told him to come in. He entered and introduced himself as Ruby's husband, Booker. She could see he was a gentle natured man and a man who had been beaten down. No doubt by the woman he was married to. He told her was glad she decided to come and visit and how he looking forward to spending time with the baby once she delivered it. Mom felt a little better knowing the other half of Ruby-Mae wasn't so bad.

Booker went on to tell her that he and Ruby ran a boarding house for Men. They housed ten men in the basement and cooked two meals, breakfast and dinner. He went on to tell her to make sure she stays on Ruby's good side because she has a quick temper and can be very combative. Booker asked, "How is the baby's father (my dad) and will he be coming to visit later?" My mom responded, "he will." I just don't know when. She went on to explain that when she left Houma she didn't tell her husband or leave a note telling him where she was going. She said, I know my husband, he was content with the life we had together in Louisiana. He was a simple man and very content with the bare essentials in life. She stated he has been conditioned by his family to believe that his place was with them forever. He believed it because that's all he had ever known. Booker told her he had a similar life too as a young man and that he would look at pictures in books about city life and all it seemed to offer. Booker told mom not to give up on dad and that he would find a way to be with her. He told her there comes a time in a man's life when he will turn away from the things he knows when he finds the one he wants to be with for the rest of his life. Mom found comfort in Booker's words and hoped he would be right because she wanted to be with my dad for the rest of her life.

The next day she was sitting in the living room gazing out the window and the boarders were out working their various jobs, Booker and Ruby went shopping for supplies and food. The phone rang she picked it up and said, "Hello" and to her surprise it was Dad. He said, "I'm downtown in Detroit" and asked how do I get to the house? She was so excited but had no idea where she was. She told him to hang on to allow her to go next door to get the address and name of the city. She bolted out the door and ran across the street to a neighbor who she was watching doing yard work. She ran up to the man and asked, "What is the name of this street and the city?" He told her you are in Ecorse, Michigan and this is Thirteenth St., and your address is above your door. She ran back to the house picked-up the phone, gave Dad the street address and name of the city. He asked, "How far are you from the train station?" My mom had no idea about the distance. He chuckled, and said, "OK I will see you shortly and he hung up the phone." A short time later, Booker and Ruby returned home. Mom was beaming with joy and told them that my father had arrived and was in route to the house. Booker yelled, "Alright! I told you he be coming soon." Ruby on the other hand looked pissed and saw it as another mouth to feed and immediately asked Mom where is planning to stay? She said, "he can stay in my room." Ruby replied, "Ain't no other man staying in any rooms upstairs, he will have to sleep in the basement with the other men." Mom was ready to cuss her out but quickly realized and remembered what Booker told her a few days ago. She agreed, and said, "OK no problem."

# THE UNKNOWN

A few hours later Dad pulled up to the house in a yellow cab. He got his luggage out of the cab and proceeded up to the front door and rang the doorbell. Mom heard the doorbell and became blushed with excitement and threw herself into his arms and they hugged each other for what seemed to be hours. Booker and Ruby came in to meet and greet him. Booker grabbed his bags and asked James (dad) to please follow him. They proceeded downstairs to the basement area where Booker had set up a cot in a little room next to the utility closet. Booker said this is the best I can do for you, Dad was happy to have a place to lay his head and he told Booker, "thank you." Dad looked at Booker and said, "I am going to go back upstairs for a minute to thank your wife for looking after my wife and child to be and then I am coming back down to take a quick nap."

So, he went upstairs to the kitchen area where Ruby was preparing dinner for the boarders. Dad said" "thank you Ruby for allowing us to be here until I can find a job and find a place to live." Shortly after they all sat down at the kitchen table and had dinner. After dinner Dad told everyone he was extremely tired from the 18 hour trip and he needed to rest. He excused himself from the table and went back downstairs and climbed in his cot and slept until early the next morning. It was about 5:00 am and he got up and a very negative spirit overwhelmed him. He knew he couldn't stay there long. He walked out of the room he was staying in and noticed all the people sleeping on cots scattered about the basement. He quietly went to the bathroom and showered, shaved and dressed. He heard movement upstairs so he went up. He found Booker preparing breakfast. He asked Booker if he knew of any places hiring. Booker responded by asking "what kind of work are you looking for James"? Dad shrugged his shoulders saying, well I would like to go to work for one of the Big Three. Bookers told dad those car manufacturers aren't hiring any nigga's. Dad was shocked to hear that. He thought by being up North he saw the last of racism. Pops said, "Are you serious? Booker said you have to be polish to get into those factories. Dad with a look of disbelief said this is the north not the south and Booker said the hunkies from the south are the ones that are in charge at the plants. "They are the gatekeepers."

Booker went on to tell Dad you might try the gas refineries and the steel plants. Dad asked what direction are they in. Booker explained he could catch a city bus that would take him right to them but, dad was conscience of the amount of money he had and decided he would walk instead of spending the little money he had. Dad said, "I think I will walk." Booker said, "It a far walk from here so I will take you in an hour, "ok." Dad was delighted, appreciative and was looking forward to starting work.

Ruby entered the kitchen where Dad and Booker were. Dad had a big smile on his face and said good morning Ms. Ruby. She turned towards him and said, "what in the hell is so good about it and why are you so happy?" Dad was shocked and realized he really needed to get a job and quick. Ruby went to tell him to get out of her kitchen while breakfast was being prepared. Booker jumped in and said to Ruby, "why are you so dam mean in the morning?" This young man was just asking a few questions about where to go to find a job. Booker and Ruby started arguing and Dad slipped back to his domicile in the basement. After about an hour or so Booker called for Dad, "Are you ready to? He responded, "yes I am." They left the house and got in the car and drove off. Booker began to tell Dad the same thing he told Mom when she first arrived.

They arrive at River Rouge Steel Mill. Dad went inside to the HR department. They handed him an application and he asked if he could take it home to fill it out and they said no. You have to fill it out here. He was embarrassed and overwhelmed with fear. He handed the application back to the receptionist and said, "I am sorry but I left my glasses at home. I will come back tomorrow. Pops didn't where glasses, he was illiterate when it came to reading and writing. He walked outside and fear overwhelmed him, he thought to himself I can't read or write what am I going to do? He realized things are much different here than back home. Back at home he would just ask for a job and the receptionist would fill out the application for you. He only had a second grade education and for the first time in his life he felt inadequate. He was ashamed and went back to the car and told Booker they weren't hiring. He hated to lie but shame had just consumed him.

They went to the Marathon Oil Refinery on Fort Street and Shaffer Road in Southwest Detroit. It was about five miles from Booker's house. Again, he went inside and this time he asked if he could have an application and this time the process was different, he was given the application to take home. He and Booker spent the rest of the day going to different factories getting applications. Later that evening they arrived back at the boarding house. It was around dinner time. Ruby was on another rampage with another boarder. Dad could hear her from outside the house. Mom came to the door to greet him. He asked her to help him fill out the applications he and Booker had retrieved that day from various factories. They spent the rest of the evening filling out applications and looking forward to getting their own place and away from Ruby.

The next day Dad was up early waiting for Booker to start cooking breakfast so he could ask if it would be possible to go back to the places they went yesterday to return the applications. When he heard movement upstairs he went up and Ruby was in the kitchen instead. He said good morning she turned towards him and said, "I don't like you nigga with your high yellow red head ass." She went on to say, "You better have a job by the end of the week or you are going to have to leave."

"I don't want you here." He was confused and caught off guard. He started thinking to himself what had he done to this lady to cause her to say what she was saying. He reluctantly said, "yes ma'am I will do my best." Deep down he was truly offended but he kept his cool because he was literally at her mercy. He started praying that God would move quickly to get him out this situation. Booker entered the room and said, "James did you get your applications filled out." Dad responded, "Yes." Booker said. "Ok we will leave in an hour or so." Ruby turned and said, "You ain't taken that nigga nowhere in my car." Booker became irate and an argument ensued between them again. Dad went back downstairs back to his room. A few hours later Booker came and told him I am borrowing my neighbor's car for the day. We can leave in a few minutes. They left shortly afterwards to submit all the applications they had gotten the day before.

While submitting the application Dad asked each potential employer, "How long would it be before someone would call." They all responded, "it could take weeks maybe even months." This was not a good sign he thought to himself. He knew he couldn't stay with Ruby much longer.

The next few weeks he was going to different places in the neighborhood looking for immediate work. He was used to doing real man's work, back breaking work or fieldwork. Because of his lack of education he stayed away from office buildings or supermarkets etc. Time was moving forward fast and his desperation was growing. He decided to go to Ruby and asked how much will you charge me to stay here monthly." Thinking this is what she wanted. She responded, "It will cost you one hundred dollars a month, twice the amount she charged everyone else." He had three hundred dollars and it was mid-July with no job in sight and winter was just around the corner which he heard about the harshness of. Agreeing to her terms and continuing to leave every morning looking for employment. Some days he would walk 15 miles going from place to place. No one was hiring. Now late August and the baby was due in a month, his money was low and the need for a job was ever increasing. A few days later he was outside helping Booker with some yard work. A friend of Bookers came by to chat. Booker introduced Dad to him. His name was John. John had a little hustle of cutting grass in the summer time and moving snow in the winter. Booker asked John if he needed any help and he replied, "yes but only every other day." John asked Dad if we would be willing to except that and Dad said, "Yes." John went on to tell Dad he could only pay him fifty cents per yard. Dad didn't care he thought in his mind he was happy of the thought of having consistent work. So he started with John the next day.

After about a week or so of working with John, Dad asked John when will I be getting paid? John said, this Friday. That Friday afternoon John pulled up and Dad went out to meet him. John gave Dad this sob story about how he had expenses that he needed to pay and he would pay him next week. My naïve Dad said, "Ok." John said I will pick you up on Monday and my Dad agreed. Monday came and no John. Tuesday came and no John. Now Dad knew this guy wasn't coming back and was not going to pay him for the two weeks of work he did for him. This was his first major lesson about life in the big city. He had never dealt with swindlers before. Being from a small town where everyone knew each other and if someone said they would do something it was done. My Dad grew up knowing his word was the most important and valuable asset he had. He was taught by his parents at a very early age that if you say you are going to do something, do it. Let the honor of your word speak for you.

*James 5:12 But above all, my brethren, do not swear, either by heaven or by earth or with any other oath. But let your "Yes" be "Yes," and your "No," "No," lest you fall into judgment.*

As time was moving forward Ruby's hatred toward my Dad was growing. This wicked spirit in her would not allow her to rest until she got rid of Dad. It had gotten to point that she would find something negative to speak about him every day. Mom now about to deliver her first baby (me) started to worry about their future in Detroit. She grew weary and depressed. She had no idea that things would be so tough and was starting to regret leaving Houma. She knew her husband was a hard worker and she knew he was doing everything in his power to provide for her and her child and he didn't deserve the criticism he was getting from Ruby. It was now October eighth, 1958 and her water broke. Dad was out doing little odd jobs every day and she had no way to contact him. By happen stance that day he was working just around the corner at a deli sweeping the floor and stocking shelves, he decided to go and check on his wife during his lunch break. When he entered the house Booker said, "I am glad you are here, your wife's water broke and we are taking her to the hospital." We called an ambulance and they rushed her to the nearest hospital. Booker and Dad left immediately for the hospital. After 12 hours of contractions and I wasn't turning in her stomach the doctors realized I was in distressed. They decided to do a C-section. I was born shortly after weighing five pounds six ounces. I had yellow jaundice and was severely under nourished. Mom was doing well and they released her three days later. I had to stay in the hospital for another seven days.

The night Mom got back to the boarding house Ruby said to her, "The reason that baby is still in the hospital is because of that no good yellow 'nigga' you got." Mom couldn't hold her peace any more. She had enough of this woman talking bad about her husband and told Ruby, "If you say another word about my husband you will never see our baby." That shut her up for the moment. Ruby never had children and the possibility of having a child in the home was something she looked forward to.

While I was in the hospital Dad found a job at a carwash near the railroad tracks. This railroad track separated the Blacks and the Whites neighborhoods, like in so many other cities back in that era. He made one dollar & fifty cents a day plus tips. He thought the tips would be great, not knowing Black folk during that time didn't tip. Nevertheless he thought things were looking up. A few days later I was out of the hospital and back at home with Mom. It was getting cold in Detroit, leaves were falling off the trees and the grass was dying and ground was getting rock solid.

One night Dad came back to the boarding house after a long day of work. He walked in the door and was struck with an iron mallet across his head. Ruby had been waiting for him hiding in the dark. She split his head wide open. He fell down the stairs unconscious in a big pool of blood. The boarders all gathered around him screaming, "Call an ambulance." They did everything they could to stop the bleeding and to keep him comfortable until the ambulance arrived. When Mom heard all the commotion she ran to where the activity was near the side door of the house. She saw my Dad laying there in a pool of blood and she ran to them asking what happened and no one spoke up even though they knew Ruby did it. The ambulance came about five minutes later and rushed Dad off to the hospital. He had lost so much blood they didn't know if he would make it or not.

*Psalms 37: 12-14 The Wicked plots against the just, And gnashes at him with his teeth. The Lord laughs at him, For He sees that his day is coming. The wicked have drawn sworn, And have bent their bow, To cast sown the poor and needy, To slay those who are of upright conduct.*

Mom insisted to the paramedics that she ride with her husband to the hospital. The nearest medical emergency room was Outer Drive Hospital which was about 5 minutes away. Mom held Dad's hand while listening to the paramedics call in the emergency room with Dads vitals. The paramedics were moving without haste, tearing open bags with syringes, gauges and IV's at a frantic pace. When the vehicle pulled up to the hospital there were four men waiting to retrieve him from the vehicle. Once they got him out they rushed him straight to surgery. Mom follow holding her stomach in pain where the stiches were from her C-section that she had just a week ago.

After Dad had been in surgery for two hours the Doctor came out to speak with Mom. The doctor said, "Ma'am your husband is one of the strongest willed men I have ever seen."

"He lost a lot of blood and his skull was literally cracked and the brain was exposed."

"He was turning purple which meant he had stopped breathing but somehow he started breathing again."

"His skull will have to heal on its own and we have closed the wound."

"We will have to keep him under sedation for at least 24 hours to give his body a chance to start healing."

"Please go home and we will let you know if there are any changes."

Booker walked in the emergency waiting room with me in his arms. He handed me over to Mom and said, "I think this young man is hungry." She went in to the waiting area and started breast feeding while starring at the wall with a constant flow of tears rolling down her cheeks. Booker said, "Barbara I am so sorry for my wife's actions." Mom said. "I can't stay there any longer Ruby is crazy." Booker asked, "where are you gonna go."

"Please think about your son", Booker said. "It's getting cold and you need to have roof over your head." Mom said to Booker, "what about my husband, I put him in this situation and caused this to happen to him." Booker replied, "I have a cousin named Earline, James can stay with her until he gets better." She looked at Booker and said, "Ok." She liked and trusted Booker. Booker gave a big hug and tried to comfort her by saying, "it going to be alright." They left shortly after and went back to the Boarding house.

# FAMILY TIES

The next day Mom calls her family to inform them of what had taken place last night. She told them how Ruby had jumped Dad and hit him with a steel mallet and how Ruby hated him from day one. She also expressed how badly Dad was injured. For the first time the uncertainty of their future weighed heavily on her shoulders and her family could hear her crushed spirit over the phone. Not wanting to run up Ruby's phone bill, she told them all I love ya'll and miss ya'll and I will talk to you later.

Her brothers and sisters were furious because they knew James was one of the most, gentle natured men they had known. They had the upmost respect and love for him. Mom's oldest brother Tom said I am going to be by his side and his brother Alton yelled I am going with you. Tom was nineteen years old. Alton was seventeen years old and had just finished high school. They were both working at the South-Down Sugar Cane Mill in Houma, Louisiana and hated every minute of it. Tom saw this as an opportunity to help his sister and to also get away from the depressive and oppressive southern way of life. He had often boasted about how proud he was of his sister and new brother in-law for having the guts to step out into the unknown to follow their dreams. He was determined to do the same. Tom had a chip on his shoulder and was very hot tempered. He was ready to do some damage to whoever hurt his brother in-law. Mom's mother and father encouraged their sons to go and try to help their daughter and son in-law. Both Tom and Alton quit their jobs at the mill and planned for their journey to Detroit. Facing their fears, a few days later Tom and Alton boarded the same train their sister and brother in-law boarded heading up North not knowing what to expect. They just knew it was the right thing to do.

After Mom had finished her conversation with her family, Ruby came out of her bedroom. Mom said to her, "Why did you hit my husband?" Ruby stood and looked at her ready and armed with another lie, she said, "I thought he was burglar."
"I heard someone walking around outside and I didn't know who it was." She went on to say I told the police everything. "That man (Dad) shouldn't have trying to be so sneaky." Mom said, "What do mean sneaky?" He's coming home from work like he has for the last couple of weeks. "You know he doesn't get off until nine o'clock p.m. and it takes him about 30 minutes to get here on foot."
"Ruby you are 'full of shit'," mom said. "You were looking for an opportunity to hurt him and you did."
"You are a sick old dried up ass bitch!"
"You bully everybody including your husband."
"What did my husband ever do to you to make you want to hit him with a dammed mallet?" Ruby was taken by Mom's harsh words and language. It's been a long time since anyone stood toe to toe with her dishing out what she usually gave. Standing in a fighting posture Mom's was ready to haul off and hit her. Booker came and asked Mom to calm down. He said to Mom, "Let's go in the room so we can talk. Mom was crying and shaking while caressing me in her arms. They entered into the bedroom and Booker told her he had contacted Earline

and she agreed to allow my Dad to stay with them until he gets on his feet. Mom asked if they had room for her too and he said, "no." He said, "Barbara you will have to stay here and don't worry I will make sure you are ok." Mom felt no comfort with his assurances regarding her safety because she knew he had very little backbone in regards to him standing up to Ruby. Everyone in the neighborhood knew she was in control of that household. Ruby often treated him with no respect and often would disrespect him in public and he never ever tried to reclaim his dignity in public or in private by what she saw the four months she had been with them.

Mom agreed with Booker and told him she needed to take a nap and that when she awoke she needed to go to the hospital to see her husband. He told her he would take her whenever she was ready.

Later that evening Mom awoke and got herself ready to visit Dad at the hospital. Ruby was feeling guilty about what she had done to my father, so she asked Mom if she could look after me while she went to the hospital. With reluctance she said, "yes." Then she told Ruby, "I appreciate you looking after him," and shown her where the diapers and milk were and left shortly after with Booker. They arrived at the hospital a few minutes later. Mom was full of trepidation while walking toward the hospital her knees felt like they going to buckle at any moment. She just knew the doctors had bad news regarding his recovery. They went to the information desk and asked for his room number. The attendant informed them that he was in intensive care and still sedated. They went to the room and found him lying in bed with his whole head bandaged. She could only see his eyes and nose. He was breathing without the aid of a machine and that brought her a little comfort. The Doctor arrived shortly after to give her his prognosis. The doctor wasn't sure what to expect. Remember that medicine was not as advanced as it is today so the only comfort he could really give was that they had to wait and see. He went on to say that all of pops vitals were good. He said, "Mrs. Clay from my experience with injuries like this, it may be months before he is back on his feet depending on if he's able to speak and move when he awakes."

"He went on to say we just won't know until he awakes." Mom was sad she felt a calmness come over her and a voice that said, "he going to be alright." She knew it was God and she knew he was going to be ok. When the doctor left the room she started praying and thanking the Lord for the word she had received.

*Psalm 30:5 Weeping may remain for a night, but rejoicing comes in the morning.*

*Psalm 34:18 The Lord is close to the brokenhearted and saves those who are crushed in spirit.*

*Psalm 37:39 The salvation of the righteous comes from the LORD; he is their stronghold in time of trouble. NKJV*

Word about what happen to my Dad had gotten to his family back in Houma. They called the hospital room where Dad was while Mom was there. She picked up the phone and it was my Dad's father. She was not ready to try to explain the events that took place the night before. He asked Mom what happen to his son. She told him what happen with apprehension, "knowing the conversation was going to only get worse the longer she had them on the phone." Granddad

(Dad's father) went off and started to blame her for what happen to his son. She didn't want to argue with him and politely said, "if you are going to sit here and continue to cuss at me I will hang up this phone and you will have wait until he calls you, which might be a while." Suddenly the phone went dead. She knew he had hung up. Sam (Dad's Father) was not use to not being controlled or being threatened.

"Barbara", a frail voice spoke. She turned towards the hospital bed. Dad was looking at her, gesturing with his hand to come closer. She grabbed his hand and asked, "How do you feel?" He responded, "I feel ok." He was still under the anesthesia and was feeling comfortable. She said, "I am sorry James."

"I realize now I should have stood up to Ruby when she made the first negative comment towards you."

"If I had of shown more backbone in the beginning I don't believe she would have gone this far."

"I am so sorry for not standing up for you earlier." He looked at her with tears in his eyes and told her, "It's not your fault."

"She is a mean and evil woman and I don't blame you for what happened."

"It's over now I forgive her and I have to move forward." He said. "I don't know where I will stay now I can't go back to that house."

"Maybe we should go back home." Mom said, "I found a cousin you can stay with until you get better." He look at Mom and said, "at this point after what I have had to endure the last five months I am not feeling a lot of love for your relatives here in Detroit." She told him that the doctors recommended he stay in bed until his wound heals. He turned his head and closed his eyes once more and dozed back off into sleep. She pulled up a chair and stayed by his side the rest of the day. Booker had been in the waiting room sleeping. He came into Dad's room and said Barbara, "it's mid-night we have to go."

"I will bring you back tomorrow morning to spend time with him."

Tom and Alton were in Memphis Tennessee. A Porter was walking through the cars informing everyone that there was a big snow storm in Kentucky and that tree's, power lines and debris were covering tracks ahead. He said, "the train will be delayed for another day because they couldn't get a crew out to move it until the weather breaks." Alton said, to his brother "we should go out and see a little of Memphis." Tom said, "we can go get something to eat but that's about all we should do."

"They may get the tracks cleaned up earlier and we don't want to miss our train." It was after mid-night when they departed the train. One of the porters told them to be careful and that there was a strong Klu Klux Klan presence in town. The conductor told them of a place a few blocks away that served black people but you had to enter through the back door. When they left the train station the racial slurs started. White folks were yelling from their cars "go home nigga's". "It's after dark." They were unaware of the rules in the city. With fear coming over them Tom said, "we should turn around and go back to the station." Alton responded, "we are almost there and I am hungry." So they continued. A few moments later they saw the place the conductor had told them to go to. They slipped into the alley and knocked on the backdoor. A white guy came to the door and said, "what do you nigga's want?"

"Ya'll must not be from around here."

"Don't you know its pass your curfew?" Uncle Tom was offended and told Alton let's get out of here. Alton on the other hand told his brother it will only take a minute to get something. Alton ordered a sandwich and Tom declined to buy. Tom told Alton you know they may put anything in your sandwich. We should get out of here bro. Alton thought about it and said, "your right." So they walked away. When the worker at the bar returned to the backdoor and saw they had left he called the police. A few moments later Tom and Alton were stopped moments away from the train station. The cop called them over to the car and asked if they had ordered food and left before cancelling the order. My uncles looked at each other in disbelief and said, "yes." Tom told the officer that the man who took their order was rude so they left. The officer told them they could do one of two things either give me 10 dollars each or go to jail. My Uncles were furious but they didn't want to go to jail so they paid and hurried back onto the train. Sober from their experience both said they would never go to Memphis ever again.

Early the next morning the doctors entered Dad's room to check on his wounds. He was lying awake when they entered. One of the doctors asked if he was in pain. He told them he was ok and feeling a little head headache but it wasn't too bad. Before the nurses unwrapped his bandages the doctor had the nurse gave him a little more pain medicine to put him at ease before removing the bandage from his head. After they removed the bandage they discovered he was healing very fast. They expected his wounds to take months to heal. They were amazed at how rapidly his wounds had healed. Dad asked, the doctors to release him. They looked at each other and said, "Mr. Clay you need to stay for a few more days." He replied, "I need to get back to work I can't stay here any longer."

"I have a child and wife I have to provide for."

"They don' t eat if I don't work." The head doctor said, "Mr. Clay we will get back to you later today." The Doctors cleaned his wounds and re-wrapped his head and departed from the room.

Mom was up early getting me washed and fed before she and Booker went to the hospital. She heard the phone ring. Booker yelled out, "Barbara" "you have a phone call." Hello, "this is Dr. Bryant." He said "good morning Mrs. Clay." Mom responded, "I am ok," "how is my husband Dr. Bryant?" Dr. Bryant informed her that Dad seemed to be healing exceptionally well. The reason I was calling is to ask you if you would be able to care for him. She said, "of course I can care for him why would you ask me that she exclaimed." Ma'am I spoke to him this morning and he indicated you just had a baby and I know that is a full time job and I just want to make sure you will be able to change his bandages and watch to make sure he doesn't sleep too much. She said, "sleep to much?" He said, "yes." The Dr. went on to explain that with a head injury like the one my Dad suffered, that it is important he stays awake for at least 12 hours a day to make sure he doesn't slip into a comma or something of that nature. She paused and said, "if he is not out of danger why is he coming home?" The Dr. said…"well ma'am he requested to come home."

"It's against my better judgment but he indicated his absence from the home would put a hardship on the family and I understand that." She sighed again not knowing what to say…"Dr. I will be there in the hour, let's talk then." He said, "ok we will talk when I see you later this morning."

After hanging up the phone Mom turned to Booker and said, "are you sure cousin Earline will take my husband in until he gets better?" Booker responded, "Absolutely", Mom said, "Ok then let stop by Earline's house before going to the hospital." Booker looked at her and saw the worry on her face and said, "ok we can do that she lives a few blocks away." It was about 9:00 am. Ruby again offered to keep me while Mom went to the hospital to visit Dad.

As they pulled up to Earline's house, Mom was looking all around as if she was a building inspector. She was carrying the guilt of Dad's tragic experience with her. She thought to herself that she wouldn't be able to live with herself if she put him in anymore harm's way. Ms. Earline came to the door. She had a big beautiful smile and Mom could tell instantly she was nothing like Ruby. Ms. Earline instantly put Mom at ease and she eventually let her guard down. Mom explained everything that happened and assured Ms. Earline she would be at her house everyday cooking and caring for Dad. But, Ms. Earline said to her "Baby don't worry about that."
"We will do everything possible to keep your husband comfortable."
"As you can see I like quiet," Mom noticed the house was very peaceful and clean. She could smell dinner on the stove, collard greens, sweet potatoes uummmm! The house smelled so good. She thanked Ms. Earline and apologized for the quick departure and soon left heading to the hospital.

While heading to the hospital she felt comfort come over her because she was confident that when Dad left the hospital he would be in good hands. A huge burden was lifting off her shoulders. When they arrived at the hospital Dr. Bryant was in the waiting area talking to another family. When he finished speaking to the family he walked over to Mom and Booker. She told Dr. Bryant that if he was going to release Dad from the hospital it wouldn't be a problem. Then Dr. Bryant told Mom he would like to keep him under observation for one more day. He expressed how confident he was for a complete recovery and how remarkable Dad responded to the treatments earlier that morning. We moved him Mrs. Clay to a standard room. We took off all monitoring equipment and hopefully he will eat and go to the bathroom today. If he does those two things he will definitely be home tomorrow. Booker expressed how good that would be.

They all went up to see Dad. He was awake and alert. The doctor checked his reflexes and then departed the room. Mom told Dad that he would be out tomorrow and that she spoke to a cousin who would allow him to stay until he recovered fully. Dad told Mom he was intending to go back to work the next day and that he wasn't staying with no one. He just didn't feel comfortable with that. She asked, "Where will you stay?" He shrugged his shoulders and just responded, "I will figure something out." They spoke a few more hours before he went back to sleep. It was now about dinner time and she thought it might be a good time to go back to the house to check on her child. Then the phone rang, she picked up and it was her brother Tom. "Hey sis we are here at the train station," Mom shouted, "where are you?" Tom responded, "We are here in Detroit." She was just beside herself and woke my father.

She asked, "Why didn't you let me know you were coming." She gave them the address and Booker interjected and said, "I can go and pick them up and take them over to Earline's home." Mom said, "ok I will stay here with James."

"Can you bring them by here before taking them to Ms. Earline's?"

"Sure" said Booker.

A little later Tom and Alton walked into the hospital room. Their eyes were all watered up and they all gave each other a hug. Tom asked, "How much longer will James be in here?" Mom responded, "he should be out tomorrow." She told them he just dozed off again let me wake him. She woke him and he was so happy to see familiar faces he started crying. He could not believe that they had traveled all the way to Detroit to be by his side. A new love spawned within him for Mom's family. They sat and talked for hours. Tom said, "we have to find a job." Dad said, "you all can work at the car wash with me." He told them how he had been all over the city looking for employment and how he had applications submitted and hadn't received one call from anyone yet. They agreed and said, "Ok we will go over with you tomorrow."

Mom called Earline and asked if her brothers could stay for the night. Earline gladly accepted and told her to bring them right over. When they arrived Earline had dinner sitting on the table for all. She said I know you must be hungry and tired. Earline said, "I have to go to work tomorrow so help yourselves to the food and I put bedding downstairs in the basement for you both." They responded, "thank you ma'am we appreciate it very much," and she then retired for the evening. Shortly after Mom stood up and said, "I have to get back to my baby."

"I will see you tomorrow morning!"

The next morning Dr. Bryant called and said Dad was being released at noon. Mom went down stairs and gathered all of Dad clothing and things and brought them up to her room. She didn't want to be away from her husband but she had to think about the baby. She didn't know how things would pan out but was comforted by the fact her brothers were there to help. Tom called Mom and asked what time will you be picking up James from the hospital? She told him the hospital had just called and said they would be releasing him at noon. Do you know where the carwash is he asked? She said, "no but I can find out." She asked Booker and he said, "I can run them by there in a few minutes." Mom told Tom what Booker said and he said, "Ok." Booker went and picked up the brothers then took them to the carwash. They went in and asked the owner if he had openings and he said, "yes." They told the carwash owner what happen to Dad and the owner said, "I was wondering what happen to him."

"It wasn't like him to miss a day." He was the best worker I had. Is he coming back the owner asked? They responded, "yes." The owner told them they could start today. They both took off their coats and started working immediately. Booker told them he would be by later to get them after he picked up my dad from the hospital.

The hospital released Dad a little early. He was sitting in the lobby waiting for Mom. She pulled up and they departed. While in the car Mom said, "I am taking you over to Earline's." He said, "Ok but I am just going to change clothes." Then he asked, "Where are your brothers?" She told him Booker took them over to the carwash and they started working this morning. Then Dad said, "After I get changed that's where I am going too." Mom said, "I don't think that a good idea with your head still bandaged like that." His response was I will wear a hat. She knew that there was no way she was going to change his mind.

After changing into some clean clothing Dad went to the carwash to join his brother in-laws. They made a pact that day to always look out for one another. After the shift was over Tom and Alton said, "we are back to Ms. Earline's." Dad said, "I am not going." They asked, "where are you going?" He told them I don't know maybe I will sleep in the back of the building. The brothers said, "if you stay here then we are staying with you."

"We take care of one another." From that day forward they slept in back of the carwash for a month straight in the freezing cold. Alton or Tom would go by Ruby's once a week to give my Mom money for food and diapers. They put their money together and saved for an apartment. One month later they all found a little place and moved in together.

# A MAN'S MAN

A year later Tom, Alton and Dad separated and went their separate ways. Tom started a job at a small parts manufacture and Aton went into the Air Force. Dad met a man who really liked him, his name was Mr. Hicks. Mr. Hicks was a family man and a hardworking man. He was an older gentleman and for some reason he took a liking to Dad and wanted to help him out. Dad was working a night shift a cement plant at the time not making a lot of money but was working steady. Mr. Hicks worked at the Marathon Oil Refinery where Pops had put an application in over a year ago. Mr. Hicks asked Pops if he was interested in working at the refinery and Pops responded, "Yes." One day Mr. Hicks went in to see the foreman and told him about Pops. Mr. Hicks had a lot of time on the job and had a great reputation amongst his peers. The Foreman told him to bring Dad in for an interview. The next day Dad met with the Foremen and things went well. He started the very next day. Soon after acquiring that job life for us began to get better. Dad quickly earned a reputation for being hard working. He became the go to guy when they needed projects to get done quickly and efficiently. Before long all the teams at the plant wanted him on their team because good help was hard to find. He worked there for five years. I remember he would work seven days a week and never took a vacation. He never took a sick day.

One day while working he overheard some white folk plotting to get rid of a few black's. Pops didn't know why they were plotting against these guys because he thought they were hard working guys also. Because Dad looked white the whites thought he was one of them. They would often say some cruel things about blacks behind their backs. Pops was disgusted by the way they acted and thought they were cowards because they always said these things behind their backs. He would always tell me about how they would hide their intentions and lay and watch the blacks every move so that they could build a case against them and get them fired when the whites often did the same things, like extending a break for a few minutes. Dad hated to see people mistreated. He would often come home and tell Mom stories about who got put on probation or who was fired. I remember he came home one day and said they had gotten rid of all blacks except a hand full. That was in a two year period. His tenure ended when the whites found out he was black.

One day Mom dropped him off at work and one of his co-workers saw him get out his car. A few days later while having lunch, one his co-workers said I saw you getting out of a car with some woman. The guy went on to say she sure was pretty. Dad made the mistake of saying that was my wife. He let his guard down and forgot the rules of the game. I am still baffled by that today. Word started to get around that Dad was black or married to a black woman which back in the day was just as bad. He started finding racist literature on his locker and crap inside his locker. He said he knew who the perpetrators where and wanted to beat their ass daily. A few months later when it got to the point where he just couldn't take it anymore he literally chased one of the perpetrators into the human resources department and told the guy in front of a whole department he was going to kick his ass. They fired him two days later; this happened in July of 1963.

A week later I remember my Uncle Tom came by the house and he had lost his job also. He and Dad had planned to go over the Ford Motors to get hired on at the auto plant. Ford had announced they were hiring. For almost a week straight Mom and I would drop them off at the main gate of the plant at about 6:00 a.m. I remember seeing thousands of men in line trying to get an application. What I didn't see was that there were two lines because one was a lot shorter than the other that's why I couldn't see it. Later I found out the lines were racially divided. The white line moved at a rapid pace and the applications would go to them first. That's why I only saw one line outside the gate. Both lines where headed toward a make shift little office in the middle of the parking lot. The little office was about a quarter of a mile inside the gate. That gives you an idea of how long that line was.

A week went by and they had no luck getting to the HR office. The following Sunday my father and Uncle Tom decided to get to the auto plant at 3:00 a.m., hoping to assure themselves a better opportunity to get to the office and get an application. They arrived at the plant on time and people must have camped out the whole weekend, it was jammed packed. All Black folks, I saw no white. Dad told Mom and I the weekend before that there was a line for the whites and a line for the Blacks. The Blacks were waiting until the white line finished then they would only take a hand full of blacks on. Well, this must have been my father's lucky day. He said it was about noon that day and he was eating his lunch that

Mom prepared for him and his brother in-law, when a white foreman from the plant walk over to him asked, "What are you doing in this line?" Pops was sitting talking to someone he had just met he answered, "I'm trying to get a job like everyone else here." The foreman said, "you are in the wrong line." By this time the white line had dissipated. The foreman said, "you need to follow me!" Pops said, "he got up and really didn't know what to expect and followed, they walk in the gate towards the office where the applications were being filled out." The foremen told dad, "you shouldn't be in the nigger line, you'll never get hired." Dad said he looked at that man and wanted to hit him but cooler heads prevailed and he didn't say anything, he just let the man rant.

When they arrive at the office the foreman escorted Pop's straight inside and asked the secretary for and application and handed to Pop's. Then he told him to fill it out and you will start tomorrow. Dad looked at the man and was totally blown away. The foreman took him for a white man and pops was ecstatic. He thought to himself God has just blessed me beyond my wildest dreams. The foreman said you need to fill this out now, Dad walked over closer to him and said, "Sir, I can't read or write." The foreman said, "no problem you sit down and I will ask you the questions and will fill it out for you."

*1 Samuel 2:26 And the child Samuel grew in stature, and in favor both with the Lord and men.*

*Psalm 119:58 I entreated Your favor with my whole heart; Be merciful to me according to your word.*

*Job 33:26 He shall pray to God, and He will delight in him, He shall see His face with joy, For He restores to man His righteousness.*

*Psalm 41:11 By this I know that You are well pleased with me, Because my enemy does not triumph over me. NKJV*

After the foreman assisted my father he asked my father how did you here get to the job site? Pops told him his wife dropped him off and the foreman replied, "I would be obliged to take you home if you can't get a ride." Dad thanked him for the offer and opportunity and told him he could get a ride home. When Pops left the jobsite he couldn't go back to the black entrance because the foreman reposted himself right outside the gate. Dad walked three miles to the nearest phone booth and called my Mom. She picked him up from the location he called from shortly after their conversation. I remember when he got in the car he asked Mom to drive by the plant to try to discover his brother-in-law. We had no success.

Later that evening Uncle Tom had finally shown up at the house. He was exhausted and asked Pops what happed to him. Pops turned around and told Uncle that he had gotten hired and was starting tomorrow. Pops was so happy maybe the happiest I had ever saw him during that time. Dad said Tom I will do everything I can to get you a job. He told him to give him a little time to get himself established first. After, Pops passed his probation and proved himself of being a good worker and dependable, he gained favor with his Foreman and peers. He asked the Foreman to hire a good friend of his. Because the Foreman was so impressed with my Dads work ethic he hired my Uncle Tom a week later.

Dad worked another 23 years straight without ever taking a vacation or sick day. He had perfect attendance for 23 years. Not too many folks can say that. His work ethic was just unbelievable. I remember as a young man he pushed me so hard. He would make me cut the grass in our yard over and over again until I would get it perfect. What I learned from those experiences was to take pride in my work. I remember when I went into the military, everyone was so afraid of the Drill Sergeants and I remember seeing the panic and fear on the faces of new recruits. I would try to calm them. I was so well prepared by my father I just knew that there was nothing they could do to me that I wasn't ready for. I knew they couldn't work me as hard as I was driven as a young man. I skated through boot camp. I thank him often for being the man that he was and for being my earthly father. He set a great example for me to follow.

I remember when family would come by on the holidays Dad would get so many praises from people for just being a good man. Mom's friends would always tell her that they wish they had a man like him. A man that always meant what he said. If he told someone that he was going to do something, there was no need to worry because he would get it done no matter what was going on in his life. Everything came second to his word.

*James 5:11-12 Indeed we count them blessed who endure. You have heard of the perseverance of Job and seen the end intended by the Lord—that the Lord is very compassionate and merciful. But above all, my brethren, do not swear, either by heaven or by earth or with any other oath. But let* your "yes" be "yes," and your "no" be "no," lest you fall into judgment. NKJV

His carried himself with the upmost character. He was a man of honor and dignity. He treated everyone with respect as long as it was mutual. He was a leader not a follower. When I was young I would often hear him say "do not be a follower, "be a leader." I am so glad he taught me that. He would tell me followers always finish second and they never develop a personality of their own. He would tell me if you become a follower you will make the same mistake as everyone else and that you will never be able to trust what you think is right. That was a very wise statement and truth. He was that man. No one could give him advice but his wife because, she was the only one he trusted here on earth. He had unshakable faith in the Lord. Our Lord seemed to show up and come through for him like I have never seen.

Matthew 7:12 So in everything, do to others what you would have them do to you, for this sums up the law and the prophets. NIV

Proverbs 18:24 One who has unreliable friends soon comes to ruin, but there is a friend who sticks closer than a brother. NIV

1 Peter 2:17 Honor all people, Love the brotherhood. Fear God. Honor the King. NKJV

Dad had the ability to read people it got more pronounced later in his life. He would often sit back and observe people without interacting with them. I remember he would tell

Mom about her friends or people they would meet at a social function. He could tell if that person was a person of honor or if they were deceitful and mischievous. Mom would say, "James you don't know those people" and an argument would ensue because Mom would always claim he was being judgmental. She would have to apologize shortly after because time would past and nine times out of ten times he would be right on. He just knew.

*Ecclesiastes 7:12 Wisdom is a shelter as money is a shelter, but the advantage of knowledge is this: Wisdom preserves those who have it.*

*Proverbs 2:10-11 When wisdom enters your heart, And knowledge is pleasant to your soul, Discretion will preserve you; Understanding will keep you. NKJV*

# A MEDICAL MIRACLE

September 1, 1991, I was living in California, I received a phone call from my Mom at about 9:00 am. Mom was hysterical crying and babbling for a few moments. My mind went immediately to my brothers. During that time my younger brothers seemed to be doing all they could to bring shame and dishonor to my parents. One was on drugs and the other was on drugs and was an alcoholic. Mom and Dad would often call to vent and would ask me to come home to put them out. I really was expecting to hear something like that because it seemed to dominate all of our conversations. I rarely would hear from her during mid-day since she was three hours ahead. When she had calmed down she said, "Baby you have to come home." I asked, "Why?" and she could barely get it out, "your Dad was rushed to the hospital this morning and I don't know if he is going to make it." At that time I was dealing with several problems at home and at work. I was in the middle of an audit at work and at home lets just say I was trying hard to keep my marriage from ending, I knew that if I left it could mean that I might lose both my family and job. I didn't dwell on it for long, I remembered something my Dad would often say, "always do the right thing no matter what." In this case it was to be at his side. I knew he would have appreciated that so I had my secretary make plane reservations for an immediate departure. While on the plane I reflected back on what I was doing the year before on that day. Panic and fear overcame me.

I remembered I met my father in Louisiana last year around this time to bury his mother. Then it hit me, my father's mother died on September 1, 1990 and his father died on September 1, 1989 and he was rushed to hospital on the day his mother and father died. The tears started uncontrollably. People always said things happened in threes. What a coincidence I thought to myself. All I could do was pray and hope that I get a chance to see him and speak to him before he passed. I was frightened. Praying and weeping was all I could do, I felt so helpless during that time.

When I arrived in Detroit at about 10:00 p.m. that night, Mom was there to pick me up. She was in tears and really distraught. I told her I wanted to go straight to the hospital. She replied, "He is in intensive care and visiting hours end at 10:00 p.m." While driving home I knew I had to be strong and courageous for her. This was really the first time I had ever seen her confused not having a solution as she so many times did. She had always been the rock of the family. I realized something I had never recognized, she was the strength behind my Pops and he was her pillar. I realized also that they had a dependency on each other and a bond that was stronger than most married couples, I had ever known. I was shocked. The reason for the shock was because I hadn't really spent time with them since I left to go to college about 12 years prior. It was a bitter sweet revelation because of the occasion. That night, I stayed up with her for hours talking about how awesome Pops was and reminding her of all the trials and tribulations we have seen this great man survived and overcame, reminding her that he never gives up and that he is a fighter and a winner. I was just as frighten as she was about losing him but I knew I had to be strong for her so I never showed any signs of skepticism in front of her even though my days were darker than hers, all my problems she didn't know about.

The next day we arose early in the morning and was at the hospital at about 6:00 a.m. We happen to see Dad's physician in the elevator and I took the liberty to question him about Pops condition. He indicated your dad is fighting. Mom and I both needed to hear that. He said, "he would meet us in the room a little later after he made his rounds." We shook hands and parted. After we parted, I turned to Mom and said, "he is a very young doctor." She turned to me and said, "I like him and I think he will take good care of my husband." I remember shrugging my shoulders and saying, "Ok." I always agree with Mom. When we arrived at the room in intensive care I almost broke down and cried on the spot. Mom put her arms around me and said, "it will be alright." I gathered myself and pushed on. There was so much machinery around him you couldn't see him unless you were right upon him. I mean big machines with leads attached all over him. He was in a coma state. I immediately grabbed his hand and started praying for him. It was the first time I ever prayed publicly. I felt the Holy Spirits presence and allowed myself to be led by the spirit because I didn't know what to pray for. The words just flowed, I had no control over what was coming out of my mouth or heart. After praying I remember feeling drained, I poured my heart and soul into that prayer and made a vow to pray for him daily while holding his hand. I felt that he knew I was there.

*Romans 8:26-27 Likewise the Spirit also helps in our weakness. For we do not know what we should pray for as we ought, but the spirit Himself makes intercession for us, with groanings which cannot be uttered. Now He who searches the hearts knows what the mind of the Spirit is, because He makes intercession for the saints according to the will of God.*

*John 14:16-17 And I will pray to the Father, and He will give you another Helper, that He may abide with you forever— the Spirit of truth, whom the world cannot receive, because it neither sees Him nor knows Him; but you know Him, for He dwells with you and will be with you.*

*John 16:13 However, when He, the Spirit of truth, has come, He will guide you into all truth; for He will not speak on His own authority, but whatever He hears He will speak; and He will tell you things to come. NKJV*

Mom sat next to him and spoke to him as if they were having a conversation. She went on for hours, on the other hand I was reflecting back on the past. Dad and I hardly got along during my teenage years like so many of us. I was hard headed and would always say things like, I don't want to be anything like my father and I held on to anger for years. However, about three years prior I was 31 years of age and was really going through some tough times and I called him because I was having a reoccurring dream about a family curse and I was led to speak with him about it and no one else. I shared with him that it seemed that no matter what I tried to do I would fail. I worked hard and I always experienced setbacks and constantly had these nightmares about a curse on the family. His response that day was, as long as you believe in God the Father and Jesus Christ no harm will come to you. He never answered the question directly so I took what he said and started on a quest to find the faith that I had lost over the years. Still reflecting, I remembered a few months after that conversation I went to visit them both. I sat my Dad down in the family den and I told him how much I appreciated him and for the first time I told him that I loved him, and thanked him for never giving up on me or the family. He looked at me and said, "Son I love you too and I know I was hard on you but I just didn't want life to slap you around like it does to so many people."

"I was hard on you intentionally and sometimes I went too far." Before he could say another word I said. "no Dad you didn't go too far because I wouldn't be half the man I am today if you hadn't been so hard."

"I appreciate it now more than you will ever know." He seemed content and the burden of guilt had lifted off his shoulders and mine. It was a conversation both of us needed to have, this conversation meant more than any conversations I've ever had with anyone. I felt comforted then because if he was leaving us I knew he knew I loved him and appreciated him.

Moments later the physician entered the room. I asked, "what Dads prognosis?" "how long was he expected to be in a coma?" He went on to tell that Pops had severe liver damage. Mom knew he was sick a month ago and tried to get him to see a doctor but he refused because he didn't want to miss a day of work. The doctor told us Dad had been spitting up chunks of his liver mixed with blood. He also stated this had to have been happening for a while because of the severity of his condition. He said, "if they would have been five minutes later getting to the hospital he would have died choking on the chunks of liver that were in his esophagus."

On top of the liver damage all his organs were shutting down the kidneys, appendix, bladder, pancreas etc. The doctor just kept repeating that he was very lucky and we would have to take it one day at a time. For the next two weeks Mom and I rotated our time with him. I went in the morning hours from 6:00 a.m. to 3:00 p.m. then she would come and sit with him from 3:00 p.m. to 10:00 p.m. this way someone was with him all day.

Two weeks rolled by and he was showing little signs of improvement. The third week a staff of doctors entered the room and asked to meet with me and Mom. I set the meeting up for the next day. I thought they wanted to do another surgery but what they wanted to do was pull the plug. Mom said, "no way are you going to pull the plug on my husband." She told them he will come out of it and you are going to give him a chance to. I agreed and told them that they had no idea how strong this man was. We prayed continually.

In the third week we were still on our daily schedules and this one particular day I decided to stay with Mom during her shift. She was looking a little defeated this day and I said to her, "Mom he is going to be alright, he'll get through this." A few moments later his eyes opened and he turned and looked at Mom and tried to speak her but the breathing tubes were in his mouth. I ran out into the hall to the nurse's station saying please come quick Dad is awake. A couple of nurses ran into the room, one yelled out call the doctor quickly. The doctor was there shortly after and he checked Pops and they pulled the curtains. He told them to start disconnecting things and he was talking to Pops and he was responding. This was a good sign. Much better than they expected but exactly what we prayed for. Later that evening the doctor came and sat next to me and said, "James I really didn't expect your Dad to come out of this." He went on to say, "your Dad is one tough man, I didn't expect him to last two days." I looked at the doctor and told him not to give up on my father because he is stronger than any man I have known over the course of my life. I felt very proud to say that and from that day forward I have always said, "if I could be half the man he is then I am in good shape. He became my hero that day.

Pops still had a long way to recovery. The doctors put him on a list for a liver transplant. They had to cut out 80% percent of his liver because of the damage to it. I remember asking the doctor if I could give up half of my liver not knowing I couldn't live without it and the doctor reminded me that I couldn't live without it and that they were putting him on an organ donor list. Pops other organs were still down and the doctors were trying everything to get them back to a functioning state. Pops hadn't urinated in a while. Doc tried a procedure on his kidneys and it didn't work. I went to him again and said, "I know I can live with one kidney and we should be a match." The Doctor told me if what he was going to try next didn't work and that if I was willing to donate a kidney he would perform the procedure. I felt a need to do all I can and this wasn't a time for me to be selfish. I wanted him to live and Mom to be happy even at my expense. Doc said he was going to try to get his organs functioning with medication because of the weak state Pops was in. He couldn't handle surgery right at that time. Well, a few days later, the medication worked and Pops organs were recovering. He was on his way to recovery. Pops was talking and finally able to eat a little food which is always a good sign that recovery is well on the way.

I made reservations to fly back home that evening, knowing Pops was on a donor list and that his physician now would do all he could to keep Pops living, I felt a since of comfort and relief. After I departed, Pops stayed in the hospital for six more weeks before he went home.

# THE LORDS CALLING

After spending two and a half months in the hospital, eight weeks in intensive care and two weeks recovering Pops was finally home. A month after being home and gaining his strength he had another surgery. The doctors installed a shunt on the left side of his chest because of poor blood circulation and a malfunctioning liver. After the shunt installation Pops had to press this device at least ten times a day in order for him to continue to live.

On Friday August 13, 1993, Mom received a phone call from the hospital informing her they were in possession of a liver and wanted to schedule surgery for my Dad on Sunday, just two days later. She called me to tell me the good news. We spoke for hours about how she wanted Dad healthy again. She was frightened and I could hear it in her voice, she kept saying he has suffered so much. I consoled her as much as possible reassuring her once more that Dad is a fighter, and how important it was for her to keep her spirits up especially in front of Dad. I reminded her of what he had been through in the last year and that we have to be strong for him and that he was the only thing that mattered. She seemed to be ok with that because the tone of her voice changed from skepticism to absolute confidence that Pops would in fact come through it. Before hanging up I told her I would fly in shortly after the surgery to be with them both for a few weeks.

Early the next day Mom called again before I could call her to ensure she was doing ok because it was the day before surgery. When I answered the phone she said, "you are not going to believe this", I said, "what Mom?" She went on to say, "Do you remember Lucky?" I said, "That's my cousin and one of my Dads best friends right?"

"Yes," he died this morning," my heart dropped to my feet. My Father didn't have many friends. Lucky was someone he enjoyed being around. They would sit for hours chatting about the old days back in Louisiana and in Detroit. I knew if he had of gotten news of his death it would have set him back for sure. The confidence I had just went away. For the second time in my life I felt something I have never felt before a possibility of loss and both times it was regarding my Dad. Mom was in tears again and she asked, "what should I do?"

"Should I tell your dad?" I told her, "absolutely not."

"He has surgery tomorrow Mom, lets tell him after the surgery when he gets back home and on his feet." I went on to tell her if our family members call and want to talk to him don't let them, just tell them he's sleep or something. She agreed and I told her I would be praying for Dad tonight and before his surgery tomorrow morning and we hung up. I immediately dropped to my knees and prayed. Again, not knowing what to pray for I allowed the Holy Spirit to lead me.

The next morning Mom got Dad to the hospital at 4:00 a.m. His physician had called in other doctors from around the world to assist and observe. A team of ten doctors were present for the surgery. The operation started at 6:00 a.m.

The surgery lasted 18 hours and my Dad died 5 times. The first time he was dead for 20 minutes. The last time and final time they thought they had lost him was during a 11 minutes thirty-five seconds time span. The other three times ranged between those times. The doctors kept shocking him back. They shocked him so much that his backside was completely burned, chard. The shocking went on all throughout the surgery.

# A PRICELESS GIFT TO ME FROM MY FATHER

This is what Pops had to say about his death experience:

A man came to me and said, "James I am going to take you to the mountain top."

"You are going to see a light."

"This is a light that you have never seen on planet earth before in your life." The man went on to say, "you are going to try to look beyond that light but you won't be able to see anything."

That light was on top of a mountain across from me and I was on another mountain it seemed to be about 300 to 400 hundred yards away. I tried to look beyond that light but I couldn't see anything. I couldn't look at it, because of the brightness.

It was dark up there. I looked down and saw a valley way down. It was daylight down there, I mean it was bright, so I went to get back to get on the bed and I was looking for the man who took me to the mountain top but he had disappeared.

*Revelation 21:10-11 And he carried me away in the Spirit to a great and high mountain, and showed me the great city, the holy Jerusalem, descending out of heaven from God, having the glory of God. Her light was like a most precious stone, like a jasper stone, clear as crystal.*

*John 8:12 Then Jesus spoke to them again, saying, "I am the light of the world. He who follows Me shall not walk in darkness, But have the light of life."*

*Matthew 5:8 Blessed are the pure in heart, For they shall see God. NKJV*

Then there was a woman who came and pushed me in to a gymnasium. It was very cold in the there. It was the size of two basketball gyms and the place was packed with dead people. Dead bodies were everywhere on slabs. I looked up and saw the bodies, all with toe tags on them. The woman came to me and took the tag off of my toe and walked toward my head and put her hand on my shoulder. I looked up at her trying to see her face and she would turn at an angle so that I couldn't see her face, she kept turning away every time I tried to look at her. The woman was dressed in brown with a scarf covering her face. Her eyes and nose was only exposed. It was cold in this place. I never experienced any cold like that before. She said, "James don't worry you are not going to die."

Moments later I was in Jerusalem the Holy Land standing next to a Muslim. I was on a street standing next to bus at a bus stop. I saw Jews, Arabs and Blacks fighting, I mean crazy fighting. Everyone was fighting. It was total kaos. People were rioting and beating one another, it was crazy. They were fighting like dogs. They came and knocked me and the Muslim both down and we rolled under the bus when we stopped rolling, both of us were on our stomachs.

*Matthew 24:21-22 For there will be great tribulation, such as has not been since the beginning of the world until this time, no, nor ever shall be. And unless those days were shortened, no flesh would be saved; but for the elect's sake those days will be shortened. NKJV*

We heard a shot, like a gun shot. And there was a pain that ran through my stomach where I had surgery, like a hot flash. But after that flash of pain I had no more pain in my stomach. The pain went instantly away.

We were under the bus and there was a red flashing light (like a little bulb) running back and forward in front of me under the bus. There were about twenty to thirty thousand people standing near the sea looking and yelling at me chanting (burst the light, burst that light). They were all saying if you burst the light you will stop us from fighting. So I grabbed the light and broke it with my right hand. My hand felt like it was on fire. I got from under the bus and ran over near the sea and used my left hand to shove my hand that was on fire into the white sand. The pain went away instantly. I started crying, crying like a baby and walked over by the sea, telling everyone please don't tell no one, but I burst that light, I burst that light. Seemed like I couldn't stop saying I burst that light. Then a man came to me and gave me a Brown Robe. I put it on and instantly started preaching about Jesus Christ. I was telling them that Jesus is coming back and he will stop all this corruption. He is going to put an end to this.

Quote: "All the ones that don't have their life in order, My God I feel sorry for them, I really do".

So after I looked and saw a big hole by the sea. It was a huge deep pit. I saw a guy that I worked with for 28 years down in a pit. I still had my brown robe on. I went into the pit to make sure it was him. I tried to get his attention but he wouldn't respond as if he didn't see me. He was moving dead bodies and washing dead bodies. All the bodies he moved to the right of him were going to hell and the ones he left in place were going to see the maker. I hadn't seen him in two years, not since I left work sick.

Quote: "All the ones that don't have their life in order, My God I feel sorry for them, I really do".

I left from there and I went to a big red church. The sun was extremely bright that day. I was trying to get into the church. There were thousands of people outside trying to get in. Cars were park everywhere. It was packed. I got inside, someone said, "your cousin Lucky is here, he just joined us," saying, "the family didn't know if the body was going to be shipped back to Louisiana or not." Then someone said, "Your wife's father is here, he's been here for about ten years", I went over to the corner where they said he was and I couldn't find him. Then it got real dark, pitch black and the wind started blowing, trees were bending down to the ground, freight trains were just falling down and being snapped apart.

*Joel 2:31 The sun shall be turned into darkness, And the moon into blood, Before the coming if the great and awesome day of the Lord. NKJV*

## A Message from My Father

People were trying to hold on to anything they could. The choir started singing "Your Grace is Mercy", I had never heard that song in my life before. It was sounding so good. Then the people started yelling this is judgment day, this is judgment day. People started to panic and were scurrying to and fro, just all out panic. I stood in the middle of the crowd and yelled really loud, "Let it Come", "Let It Come" because I am ready, I am ready and I am still ready.

After that I went to Grand Calliou, Dulac Louisiana at the end of that road. For those that are familiar with Grand Calliou, you know the road ends at the Gulf of Mexico. There was a platform out in the water. Someone gave me that same Brown Robe again as I went up on the platform. It seemed like cars were lined up from here to California and people were everywhere, they came to hear me speak about Jesus Christ. I told people about Jesus Christ, all his Glory and Greatness and that if people don't get their life together they were going to be lost forever. It's real, it's real. I can still feel it.

Quote: "All the ones that don't have their life in order, My God I feel sorry for them, I really do"

*Isaiah 61:10 I will greatly rejoice in the LORD, My soul shall be joyful in my God; For He has clothed me with the robe of righteousness, As a bridegroom decks himself with ornaments, And as a bride adorns herself with her jewels. NKJV*

Shortly after that I went to my wake, the night of my wake. I didn't see any living human being. All I saw was dead people, some of them didn't have the back of their head, they were walking around talking without the back of their heads, raising all kinds of evil, evil. Blues playing, some of them were partying, blues playing.

"They didn't have the back of their head". But when they looked at me they would try to disappear trying to hide from me but, I could see them anyway. So the night of the wake, I saw a cousin named Andrew Clay he had been dead for many, many, many years. He was standing by the door, the entrance to the funeral home. I got out of the coffin and walked over to him and he said, "Hi Couz! And I said, "Hi." Then I walked back over near the coffin and sat in the big soft chair and looked at my coffin.

The next day they were going to bury me now. They pushed me into the grave yard on a slab with wheels. Their was a young man and an old man. They opened the coffin and I was laying there looking at them and listening to them. The young man looked at me looking at them, the young man kept looking at me and he put his hands on me. Then he said to the old man, "We have to take this guy back." The old man said, "What do you mean we have to take him back?" The guy is dead you see they already dug the hole. The young man said, can't nothing kill this man **"he is one of them"**. The old man came over and said, "What you mean?" Then the old man came over and touched me and said, to the young man your right, "we have to take him back, **He is one of them**."

"Nothing can kill him!"
"He is one of them!"

*John 3:16 For God so loved the world that he gave His only begotten Son, that whoever believes in Him should not perish but have everlasting life.*

*John 5:24 Most assuredly, I say to you, He who hears My word and believes in Him who sent Me has everlasting life, and shall not come into judgment, but has passed from death into life.*

*1 Corinthians 10:11 Now all these things happened to them as examples, and they were written for our admonition, upon whom the ends of the ages have come. NKJV*

As I was returning to my body I could see everything that was happening in the operating room. I slowly descended back and the doctors came to me and I started speaking to them about where I came from, what I experienced and thanked them. A team of ten doctors from all over the world looked at me with amazement. They said, "Mr. Clay we didn't save you don't thank us, God brought you back." They told me I should be in church every Sunday thanking Him and dropping a few coins in the plate because it wasn't anything they did. They called me a 'medical miracle' because no one should have survived what I had been through and if they did, they should have been a vegetable. Clinically dead for over an hour is just unheard of but I thank God the Almighty who can do anything including raising the dead. Thank you, God Almighty.

# LIFE AFTER SURGERY

The Doctor's came out to see Mom after the surgery and they were all totally amazed. One of the doctors said to her, "Ma'am I have heard of stories about people who died and lived to tell about it but I have never experienced or witness anything like I just witnessed."
"Your husband has a story to tell you that undoubtedly will be something not short of Glorious; he has seen things that we will never see." As they were talking to Mom the orderlies were wheeling Dad out of the operating room taking him to his room. His personal physician told Mom he would be sleep for the next 24 hours and to go home to rest.

Mom decided to stay in the hospital room with Pops until he woke. The next day when he came to he was doing so well they removed the breathing machine and other devises monitoring his organ functions. Dad started telling her about what he experienced. She still hadn't told him about Lucky dying just before his surgery and it was eating at her. She stopped him in the middle of his conversation and said, "James I have something to tell you" and he went on to say please let me finish. She said, "ok" and as he went on he told her that someone had told him his cousin Lucky had just died. She burst out in tears and wept without ceasing. He then started naming other people he heard about and finally told her about her father. She was devastated and immediately called me from the hospital to share with me what Pops had just shared with her about his experience. I was blown completely away and knew that every word he said about his experience was true.

I came to visit a few weeks later and he sat me down and shared his story with me. I remember feeling convicted and captivated with every word he spoke. Pops was different. From that point on he was never the same. He would look at you and you would think he was looking through you and still today I believe this was a gift he received when he was younger but now it was enhanced. My brothers experienced that they could no longer go to him and lie to him. He would tell them what they were thinking before they opened their mouth. He was simply amazing.

A few months later went back to visit him again this time to help him file his retirement papers for Ford Motor Co. I had never been inside Ford's plant before. The Rouge plant is huge. The Plant is about 23 square miles, with cobblestone streets and just about every square inch of the facility was built up. I went to HR, introduced myself and James Jr. and the response was amazing. Everyone was asking how Pops was doing. They hadn't seen him in eighteen months. I went on to tell them he was doing well. A VP came out of his office and said, "are you James Clay's son?"

"Yes, I am."

"Please come into my office." I followed him into an office and he asked me to shut the door. As I looked at him, I noticed this gentleman from a newspaper article, he was one Fords top executives, he was credited with turning the company around in the late eighties. He said, "young man!"

"I have known your Father for twenty-five years or more."

"He was a very honorable man, a man of great integrity and it was an honor to work with him." He went on to say. "I have missed him, he was someone I confided in often."

"A lot of my success was due to him."

"I want you to know that."

"I tried to bring your Dad up through the ranks with me but I could never get him to budge."

"Your Dad turned down every offer of advancement."

"He wouldn't allow me to show him any impartiality."

"I respected him so much for that." He would sit where you are sitting and have lunch with me and talk about how to make our operation run smoother and more efficiently. The guy was amazing.

You take care of your Dad, and it was nice to meet you. I shook his hand and thanked him and exited out of the office and got his paperwork and followed the foreman to Pops last job at the plant facility. I met everyone he worked with and was humbled again by the folks he worked with daily. They took me into their lunch area and again just praised him for being a man of integrity and honor. I left here thinking to myself, I want to leave a legacy just like this for my children to follow. I was so proud to be his son and I am still. His character was impeccable.

The next day I needed to take him to his UAW office (local union) to get the remainder of his paper work for retirement. We got there that morning at about 10:00 a.m. Pops was still very weak from the operation and I had to assist him getting out of the car and into the office. He asked me to take him into a conference room where the meeting would take place and said, "leave here I will be ok." Since his surgery I watched him like a hawk ensuring his immediate needs were always taken care of. I walked out of the conference room and met an old high school friend and we sat and talked for a few minutes and suddenly I heard my Pops cry out. I rushed back into the conference room where I sat him. He was crying and begging me to get him out of there. I grabbed his cane and assisted him back to the car asking him what's wrong. He just kept saying get me out of here please. We got to the car and I seated him and asked again "Pops what wrong are you in pain or something?" He looked at me and said, "you do remember the man I told you I saw cleaning and moving bodies in the pit in Hell." Yeah, you said you worked with him for 28 years. "Right, well I just found out he died six months ago."

"All that I saw Son was real."

"I know it now for sure." Pops sobbed all the way home and kept repeating "I hope people get their lives in order because they don't want to go where I have been."'

The Lord allowed Pops to be with us four more years. He always wanted to retired and move back to his home town of Houma, Louisiana. He and Mom moved back in 1996. His wishes were granted. In May of 1997 he was rushed back to the hospital again. This time he suffered a massive heart attack. Because of his weaken state and the anti-rejection organ medication, made this episode more serious. I took another leave of absence from work to spend time with him. I had to be there for him and really looked forward to another opportunity to care for him because my love and respect for him had grown tremendously over the past few years. Mom and I re-incorporated our routine of a split shift. She spent the mornings with him this time and spent the afternoons & evenings with him. On or about the forth week Pops went into a deep sleep. He slept for about 12 hours straight. I remember checking him every so often to insure he was still breathing. He seemed so peaceful. Then he suddenly woke and grabbed my arm, his fingernails were piercing my skin causing it to bleed, saying, "I seen him, I seen him." I broke free from his grip, he looked as though he had saw a ghost. His heart monitors went off and the nurses came rushing in. He kept repeating' "I seen him, I seen him." Once the nurses left the room I leaned towards him and spoke calmly, "you saw who Pops?" He looked at me trembling and shaken and said, "I saw the maker."

"I said you saw who Dad?"

"He said I saw Jesus." I said, "How do you know it was him?"

He described Jesus as:

"I could only take one glimpse he was so bright I couldn't look up at him. A radiant white light, brighter than anything I have ever seen. I saw his hair was white, pure white and wooly like yours with dark skin. His feet were on fire and all I could do was kneel before him with my face on the ground. I didn't want to leave him. His love was so great, "I felt it rippling through my bones, I've never felt anything like that before in my life." I asked him, "Can I could stay and when he spoke I had to put my hands over my ears and kept my eyes closed." His voice was so loud I could barely stand it. With every word that came out of his mouth it sounded like two swords rubbing against each other ( sshhhhh, sshhhhh, sshhhhh, sshhhhh) with every word. He (My Lord)told me I had to come back because my place was no ready. I begged him to please let me stay and he said, "James", "you still have work to do." I could see the Angels in the background all had their swords out sharpening them as if they were getting ready to do battle. Then My Lord spoke again and said "tell everyone that I am coming back soon."

"Sooner than every one thinks".

*Revelation 1:14-15 His head and hair were white like wool, as white as snow, and His eyes like a flame of fire; His feet were like fine brass, as if refined in a furnace, and His voice as the sound of many waters;*

*Matthew 16:27 For the Son of Man will come in the glory of His Father with His angels, and then He will reward each according to his works.*

I stood and looked upon my dad with utter amazement. Every word my father spoke to me went straight to my heart. It was meant for me to hear every word my Pops said. "Thank you My Lord again for using my earthly Father to minister to me."

# Would you like to see your manuscript become a book?

If you are interested in becoming a PublishAmerica author, please submit your manuscript for possible publication to us at:

**acquisitions@publishamerica.com**

You may also mail in your manuscript to:

**PublishAmerica
PO Box 151
Frederick, MD 21705**

## We also offer free graphics for Children's Picture Books!

**www.publishamerica.com**

CPSIA information can be obtained at www.ICGtesting.com
Printed in the USA
LVOW040545310312

275576LV00002B/97/P